Breaking Free From Financial Aid Prison

Experience Student Loan Freedom

Angela Howze

Table of Contents

Dedication

I am dedicating this book to the many student loan borrowers who were misled about their education; students who were told they could make an investment by borrowing for their future and given the illusion they would be able to repay the debt without distress; students who were financially illiterate and misused refunds from their colleges; students who borrowed money and had to drop out but are still stuck with debt; students who believed that loans were their only option for a college education; and lastly, students who were encouraged to borrow the maximum amount of student loans and are now in debt.

To the generations of students whose lives were altered because of student loan debt, there is hope! Also, to financial aid advisors who were doing their jobs and wittingly assisted in placing these students in bondage; *Steele and Williams revealed, June 28th, 2016*. I pray you find freedom and break free from financial aid regrets of placings so many students in bondage. Blessings!

Email: Angela@FinancialAidStrategist.com

Preface

Have you ever imagined what your life would look like without student loan debt? Is it possible that you could purchase a home with a low interest rate? Do your student loans cause a negative impact on your credit score? Has your student loan debt hindered you from achieving the American dream?   In order to break free from financial aid prison, we must understand the root cause of bondage. According to the Federal Reserve, Americans are $1.6 trillion in student loan debt and counting. How did we get there? This book will unlock the mysteries of student loan bondage and introduce a plan in layman terms with strategies for breaking free from the financial aid prison.

In 2010, the Obama administration signed the Affordable Care Act. This Act replaced the private loan sector known as Federal Family Educational Loan (FFEL) and became Direct Federal Loans. President George W. Bush and Congress developed the Public Service Loan Forgiveness Program and President Barack Obama put the plan into action. During this time people were beginning to experience the 2008 recession. Foreclosures, job loss, unemployment and multiple bailouts were prevalent. Beginning in 2010, people were told to attend college, obtain a degree, and work in the public sector. After 10 years of public service you would be eligible to have 15 years of loans forgiven. The problem with this notion was that predatory grantors, in their greed, loaned students' money that they could not afford to repay.

College is not for everyone, and many people attended just to receive refund checks, and others attended and eventually dropped out. This further placed minorities and their descendants in poverty. Why do I say minorities? According to Elizabeth Warren (2019) sixty percent of the $1.6 trillion deficit is held by African Americans. Federal Entitlements were passed out like candy. Guess who holds your loan note, makes up the interest rates, and has authority over defaulted loan rates? THE ANSWER IS CONGRESS! The grace period subsidy on all loans disbursed between July 1, 2012 and June 30, 2014 was eliminated by the Consolidated Appropriations Act of 2012. The first payment is due within 60 days. There is an option for deferment until the student completes their program or falls below half-time enrollment. Origination fees reflect adjusted amounts under sequestration, as mandated by the Budget Control Act of 2011 (see Electronic Announcement, June 6, 2018, for additional information).

Introduction

This is a workbook that reviews Student Loan Literacy and offers fundamental strategies for approaching the Public Service Loan Forgiveness Program. You will find quizzes, forms and previews of applications for your edification regarding student loan debt resolution. As a disclaimer, this material is to provide you with information in layman terms only. The choices you make are yours. If you need forms and assistance contact your loan advisor or visit studentaid.gov.

Testimonials

"Working with Mrs. Howze on my student loans was a godsend!!

She and her program walked me through it step by step, which is what I needed. The lessons were easy to follow, and she was right there when I had questions.

By going through her program, I've saved hundreds of dollars a month on my payments, refinanced my loans, and most importantly I have peace of mind knowing that my loans are more manageable."

- Dr. Turshá Hamilton
   Naturopathic Physician | Author | Public Speaker | Podcast Host

"When I met Angela, I was working for two FQHCs and had worked for one about 10 years prior. I had invested countless hours, which as a primary care physician I do not have, trying to gather information on my outstanding school loans and switching over to public service forgivable loans. It is a horribly tedious and frustrating task of which I could never successfully complete.

Within ONE week of meeting Angela the process was underway and within a months' time my Fed loan account was completely set up. Angela helped me select the right type of loan for my situation and then she literally walked me through every single online and/or hard document. She provided a thorough explanation of the process and thereby eliminated many of my trepidations. Despite our time zone differences, she has been at my disposal whenever I have questions or need assistance with my loan documents.

Not only has she saved me a great deal of man hours, she also saved me thousands of thousands of dollars in loan repayment. The fee she charged for her services was very reasonable for all the time and money I saved on what had been a very intimidating process for me. I have recommended her to several of my colleagues, doctors, dentists and others with similar student loan issues.

Angela is a godsend and I would highly recommend her services to anyone in need of assistance with their student loan(s)."

- Carla Hunter-Galbraith, MD

Student Loan Woes

"I just feel like I trapped, my fiancé won't marry me because of student loan debt"
- Anonymous

"I cannot get this debt behind me. Every year I owe more.
- Single Mom of 2 Pensacola Fl

"I was in Forbearance for 3years, my loans went up so high I am embarrassed to say"
- Anonymous

"My refund was levied, and I needed that money to fix my car, so I drive to work. I have been catching the bus in this ruff neighborhood". Now way out!
- LA, CA

"My social security check was garnished because I cosign for my granddaughter, I need my money, I am on fixed income"
- Grandmother from NY, NY

"I owe 400,000 dollars and still do not work in my field"
- Married Lady in Austin, TX

"I have been paying on this loan since 2003 and I still owe $3,900. I wish they would have explained the variable loan in full details before I click the link"
- Single Mother of New Jersey

"I thought going to college would help me to live the American Dream, instead
it is an American NIGHTMARE"
- Single Dad Collins, MS

"Borrow the MAX they said, I did and look at me know, 103,000 for a 4-year
Psychology degree that pays 11.00 an hour."
- Mother of 3 Laurel, MS

"I am only tired of being afraid of this debt, I pay my bill, I borrowed the
money. It keeps going up, I owe 66,754 and I took this loan 10 years ago.
- Single Woman in ATL

"My kids will not fall into this abyss, period"
- Married Dad of 3 Marion County, MS

"Our whole family has student loan debt; we are trying to put something in
place for the next generation. Just go to Vocational school instead"
- Anonymous

"My parents took my refund check and now I have this debt"
- Anonymous

"I wish I could give back my degrees in Business and exchange for this 183,000
of student loan debt"
- Married Mom of 4 St Paul, MN

Meet The Author

Angela Howze, Financial Aid Strategist "Coined Student Loan Expert" received her Master's in Economic Workforce Development from the University of Southern MS. She is a Certified Financial Literacy Instructor, with Certificates in Mississippi Development Council, Economic Led Council, and National Development Economic Council. Angela is a Coach and Consultant for Student Loan Borrowers. CFAA in 2020, Author, Mother and Wife. Angela believes that empowering communities with financial stability will provide people with a stronger level of playing field for economic growth. As a result, the Financial Literacy institute Inc, 501c3 Nonprofit Organization was established. In 2016, she taught ACT Preparation and Financial Literacy to Hattiesburg Public School District, Participated in Jump Start Initiatives with her nonprofit Financial Literacy Institute, INC and she received the Financial Literacy Proclamation from Mayor Toby Barker and awarded Top CEO's of 2020 from the Mississippi Business Journal .

Angela enjoys research and development while creating fruitful strategies to ease the burden of borrowers. Angela grew passionate about student loan debt and its impact on borrowers' lack of economic growth. Her newest Book, Breaking Free From Financial

Aid Prison was written to improve financial health for student loan borrowers and the next generation.

Angela Howze, Student Loan Expert, LLC
Secretary Mnuchin
U.S. Department of Treasury 2016 & 2017

Mayor Toby Barker of Hattiesburg, MS
and Angela Howze receiving Proclamation
for Financial Literacy, 2019

Angela Howze and Mrs. Ivanka Trump
FLEC Meeting 2017

Tami Jones Associate Publisher
Mississippi Business Journal
Top CEO Award 2020

Chapter One

My Story

I come from a biracial family. My mother was a beautiful, black woman from Mobile, Alabama and my father, a charming white man from SoSo, Mississippi. My Dad was 91 years old and my mother was 78 when they transitioned, and I never heard them talk about how to manage money. My mother would work double shifts as a nurse's aide and mainly used credit cards like Montgomery Ward, Sears, and J.C. Penney to purchase school clothes and household items. On the other hand, my father was a contractor who provided me with a lavish lifestyle. I grew up charging credit cards and spending money like there was no tomorrow. The lack of basic money management skills can handicap several generations if not rectified.

The American Dream for many means that you can purchase a home, start a family, and have the ideal job while living your best life. What keeps people from obtaining the American Dream? For me the answer was the lack of financial aid knowledge and the misconception regarding loan repayment. While preparing for my higher education, I was instructed by a financial aid advisor that in order to succeed in life, I would need a four-year degree and a Master's. She then recommended taking out the maximum student loan amount each semester. Feeling reluctant to borrow the money but was encouraged and assured that repayment would be easy after I finished school and degreed. So far from the truth. It was very hard to obtain a job and repay the debt.

Upon completing my education, I began to share the same misinformation with the next generation. My children have attended college and have graduated with certificates and degrees, and some are debt free. Some of them will not pay all the compounded interest because they were accepted into programs that I am going to share with you. It was hard rearing my children without the necessary resources. So, as my journey began to have my children degreed, I was thankful for resources like the Pell Grant, scholarships and merit awards that do not require repayment. I did not have the resources available to pay for my children's education, nor a college savings or 529 plan. As a result, my children became indebted to Sallie Mae. While I was thankful for the loans, I was not happy about the interests accumulating.

One by one, my children began to graduate with mounds of debt while obtaining degrees or certifications. I wanted to be excited because my children were graduating and yet, I was sad due to the chains of bondage being placed on their mental status. I said, "ENOUGH!" I began to look for ways to reduce the debt or and work on an end date of repayment. I started to strategize on how to foster a better situation for my younger children.

Before Learning Strategies

Here are 3 Target words I would like for you to understand in its entirety.

Refund - is a term that makes the student believe they have something that it owed to them. However, the refund from a student loan is debt that you have borrowed that must be paid back, and years of compounded interests.

Promissory Note - You are signing a contract to repay a debt. Read before you click and understand all of the implications.

Institutionalized Debit Cards – You get your refund, the school places it on a card and charges the student more services fees to use.

Vocational Training - May be a great option with less accumulation of student loan debt.

Read - Review the fine print on every form to avoid entrapment

Programs you should review before attending college:

- Educational Cost Estimates
- Financial Aid a. FAFSA
- Stafford Loans c.
- Parent Loans for Undergraduate Students-Stay away from if possible or only borrower what you need
- Federal versus private loans
- Grants
- Student Debt Repayment Plans-usually 25 to life of repayments be careful

I realized that optimizing my children's academia while in middle school was an option. Therefore, we practiced on achieving the following before college:

- Merit awards
- ACT/SAT merit awards
- Sports scholarships
- Glee Club
- Choir, Band
- Dual Registration
- Internships
- Entrepreneurship
- AmeriCorps
- Workforce

- Financial Literacy

Most importantly, I insisted that my children stay home while attending college to save on administration fees, cafeteria fees, and dorm fees. The athletic fees and maintenance fees will be charged regardless. They have implemented the strategies listed above and some of my children saved thousands of dollars.

College Preparation for Middle School and High School Students. Make sure your student is preparing a solid foundation for their future.

4 Years	**English**
3 Years	**Math**- Algebra 1&2, Geometry, Pre-Calculus, Calculus, Trigonometry
3 - 4 Years	**Science** – Biology, Chemistry 1&2, Physics, Botany, Marine Science
3 - 4 Years	**Social Studies** – American History, World History, American Government, American Cultures
3 - 4 Years	**Foreign Language**
1 - 4 Years	**Visual/Performing Arts**
1 - 4 Years	**Business/Academic Electives**
1 - 4 Years	**Computer Science**

Table 1: Student Preparation for Middle School and High School

FSA ID	
Password	
College Savings	
Expected Family Contribution	
Pell Grant	
SAT / ACT	
Scholarships	
Work Study	
Fed. Sup. Educational Opportunity Grant Award	
University Room and Board	
Book Fee Waiver	
Out of State Fee Waiver	
Left to Pay	
Loans (if necessary, but not suggested)	

Table 2: Before College Checklist

Notes: Write out a plan for your children's education so they do not get trapped with student loan debt: Google "Federal Disbursement Schedule" to see a snippet of it.

_____

_____

_____

_____

_____

_____

_____

_____

_____

_____

_____

_____

_____

_____

_____

_____

_____

_____

_____

_____

_____

_____

_____

_____

_____

Visit studentaid.gov. for more tools and tips

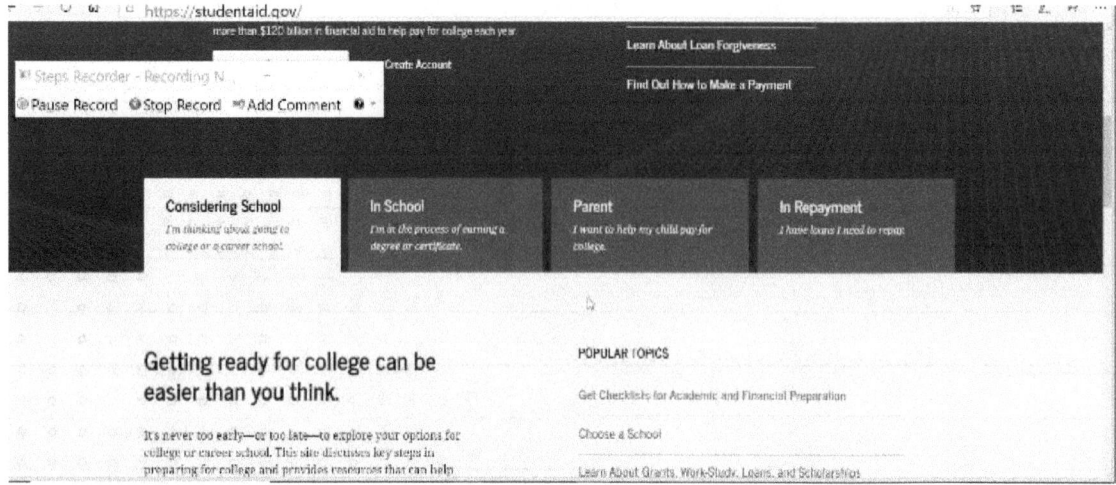

Chart 1-Retrieved from Website StudentAid.gov

Do an Education Analysis
Things you should know before attending college
Educational Cost Estimates, Financial Aid, FAFSA, Stafford Loans, Parent Loans for Undergraduate Students, Federal versus private loans, Grants, Student Debt Repayment Plans.

During College

·Continue to take ACT/SAT to obtain a higher score

·Go the WIN Job Center/Unemployment office to see if there are any grants available for your major i.e Lpn, Pharmacy Tech,Internship etc

·Sophomore/Junior Year

·Apply for Residential Assistance to cover dorm fees

Chapter Two
What is Financial Aid Prison?

To be in financial aid prison is like living with a 50-pound chain tied around your neck, constantly trying to figure out how to break free from the weight that has you burdened. The worst type of captivity that a borrower can suffer is mental debt because the interest continues to grow no matter how much you pay each month.

Many people will be paying for an education that took 4 to 6 years to achieve but will take a lifetime to pay back. The very thought of this educational debt never seeming to decrease may cause anxiety, frustration and a sense of worthlessness, not to mention the negativity it can have on your credit report or everyday life. Imagine graduating from college with over $90,000 in student loans and then you get denied when you apply for a $7,000 used car. How can that be? Forget the American Dream. Most borrowers would like to have peace, free from the agony of having mounds of student loan debt.

Yes, it is true that without student loans many people would not have the opportunity to attend college. What happened to allowing the Pell Grant to pay for a student's college education, if used correctly? I will tell you…pride. Many borrowers want to stay on campus to experience the college life, refund balling, and independence without proper life skills.

We should prepare students today with these key concepts of student loan strategies to prevent student loan borrowing. Knowing these concepts may prevent financial insecurity.

- Budgeting
- Credit
- Credit card usage
- Cash flow
- Investing
- Spending habits and communicating with money
- Predatory lending
- Home ownership
- Entrepreneur mindset and workforce
- Compounded interest
- Effects of Student Loan Bondage

I wonder how many borrowers wish they could have a do-over knowing what they know now about student loan debt? What would they do differently? Write your thoughts below:

_____

_____

_____

_____

_____

_____

_____

_____

_____

_____

During College: Learning Objectives

Knowing the history of student loan debt that you may have accrued will help you apply proven strategies to achieve financial aid freedom.

Where did this cycle of student loan imprisonment begin? Who is responsible for this broken system? I will answer this question at the end of my version of the timeline with student loan debt. Please visit every website listed to get the knowledge you need to understand how to Break Free from Financial Aid Prison. This is a Workbook, which means you must read to gain insight on what to avoid moving forward. For a list of websites to research for more information, please visit the Reference Page at the end of the workbook.

1840 -The first student loan debt was given to a group of Harvard students 27 years before the Department of Education was formed. I often wonder what Mr. Harvard would say about the Student Loan System today. The first student loans were offered to Harvard University students in 1840. During that time, they had to use collateral to pay for college tuition. One bright day someone thought of starting a student loan program. At that time, it was not as hard as it is now to pay back loans. I often wonder what those Harvard University board members would say if they knew that the student loan system that they created would imprison so many students financially. In addition, our government receives a 20% profit from this debt which further cripple's today's families. To learn more, please refer to Items 2(a) and 2(b) on the Reference Page.

1867 - The GI Bill paved the way for our Veterans to attend college. We must always honor our Veterans. To read more about the GI Bill, please refer to Item 2(c) on the Reference Page.

1958 - Birth of the Perkins Loan with low interest rates for students to pay for college. I honestly believe this the catalyst that started the predatory lending concepts. <u>To learn more about the Perkins Loan, please refer to Item 2(d) on the Reference Page</u>.

1964 - Title IV Civil Rights Act was a crucial time in America, especially if you were a minority. People with less means wanted to attend college or obtain some type of education but had little to no resources available. During this time, black men were marching with signs cast over their shoulders saying, "I Am A MAN". Civil unrest was the norm for underserved communities, a true travesty for many. <u>To read more about Title IV, please refer to item 2(a) on the Reference Page</u>.

1965 - President Johnson wanted to deal with poverty and focus on elevating the economy. My theory is that minorities were tired of not being able to attend college, and remember, this was not long after minorities were "freed". This marked the **TRIO** by President Johnson – "The Higher Education Act (HEA) created grants, loans and other programs to help students acquire education beyond secondary school". <u>To learn more about the HEA, please refer to Item 2(e) on the Reference Page</u>.

There were a lot of programs and grants derived from HEA. I have listed a few that you may know of: (1) The Pell Grant, named after a Democratic Congressman Claiborne Pell from Rhode Island; (2) National Direct Student Loan; (3) College Work-Study; (4) Supplemental Educational Opportunity Grant; (5) State Student Incentive Grant, and so many others. I have always been thankful for the Pell Grant and SEOG programs because they allow students to graduate from college without borrowing. <u>On the Reference Page, Item 2(f) which will explain an amendment which should have been in the initial process of the 1965 HEA</u>. I believe this amendment would have prevented much of the financial aid imprisonment that students continue to experience today.

1966 -Started the birth of the Financial Aid Industry. <u>To learn more, please refer to Item 2(g) on the Reference Page</u>.

1972-1990 - Sallie Mae Student Loan Marketing makes her debut. This era was an open game for predatory lenders. Banks and collection companies had control over the financial fate of many borrowers. This debt was approved by Congress in the 1990s and was supposed to educate people, but instead it did the opposite by privatizing student loans: *Eric Westervelt, NPR 11th July 2016* To learn more about Sallie Mae, please refer to Item 2(h) on the Reference Page.

So much underhandedness went on during this era of student loans. People were impersonating college loan officers to get their student loan debt: *Jonathan D. Glader New York Times March 29th, 2007.* There was marketing sponsoring cruises for financial aid officers who targeted students for loans; *Steele and Williams revealed, June 28th, 2016.* Students were borrowing loans that they could not afford to repay. Imagine people who fell into the student loan trap two years ago. They still owe a debt they may not be able to repay. *Kaitlin Mulcher, Time November 18th, 2016.*

2010 - Congress-Bush-Obama, Public Service Loan Forgiveness Program.
This program is available to assist with debt elimination for those who qualify. To learn more, please refer to Item 2(i) on the Reference Page.

"The United States government turns young people who are trying to get an education into profit centers to bring in more revenue," Senator Elizabeth Warren, D-Massachusetts, said on the Senate floor in February of 2019. "This is obscene". The federal government should be helping students get an education - not making a profit off their backs." To learn more, please refer to Item 2(j) on the Reference Page.

The fact that our own government is profiting off the backs of Americans is disheartening on so many levels. We are supposed to be the "Land of The Free".

So, who is at fault? Why do we have this debt? We can only blame ourselves for not reading the fine print and asking ourselves how we are going to repay this debt. Did we get caught up in the notion that we just had to have a college degree for employment opportunities? Were we trying to impress our peers or family? Did we rely on the government to treat Americans with dignity? Should we not have attended college, knowing we did not have a college plan nor resources available? Were you convinced that a college education would take you out of debt, but instead found that it placed you further in debt? Many of the loans are guaranteed by the federal government, which means that they can levy your accounts if you do not repay them. This can be a nightmare by way of tax levy, denial of new loans and grants, a percentage of wages, and social security garnishments.

Please refer to Item 2(k) on the Reference Page for an article regarding Navient.

2019 - Future Act- Has a lot of benefits to automate income recertification for federal student loan borrowers who use income-based repayment plans. Please refer to the reference page to read more.

Please write your thoughts below and feel free to correspond with me through email. angela@financialaidstrategist.com what are your thoughts?

_____

_____

_____

_____

_____

_____

_____

_____

_____

_____

_____

_____

Chapter Three
After College

Learning Activity

Goal of this lesson: To adopt the problem-solving mindset necessary to drastically reduce your student loan debt responsibly.

Today's Task:

1. Dealing with student loans can be stressful. Write down 3 things that can help set a positive tone for your mindset during this process. Examples include: Positive Affirmations, Goal Setting, and Personal Mantra.

_____

_____

_____

_____

_____

_____

_____

_____

Client question: Hello Ms. Angela!

Day one (mindset): My mindset regarding my student loan has been that I cannot pay it off. This debt keeps growing. I cannot manage it so I do not bother with it. I would say that I ignore it, but not in its entirety because it's there in the back of my mind. I just tell myself that I am not going to worry about or stress over it because it is beyond what I can handle. I have started paying on it and am currently on an IDR plan and I have worked for a nonprofit for 11 years and I would like to get on the PSLF plan, but I do have questions about how much of my bank account info, if any, I need to disclose to get on the plan. I want to be able to oversee when payments are made, and I don't want them garnishing my wages. I have only made two payments due to my loan being deferred in the past and because I figured that making payments that I can afford will look good on my credit report, instead of deferring the loan and never getting anywhere but further in debt. Opting into the PSLF plan so that I can make these payments count. I don't plan to be at the job I have for another 10 years so I would like to start my own nonprofit.

- By Danelle

There are many people like Danelle who are afraid of looking at their student loan debt. Whatever you decide regarding repaying your debt, do not ignore it! There is hope through the Public Service Loan Forgiveness Program that is still available.

Danielle must begin by pulling her National Student Loan Data Sheet to see what type of loans she has from NSLDS.Ed.Gov.

Second, Danelle and you would need to determine the best repayment plan options on studentloans.gov. Login and click the "Manage my loans" in the top right hand corner. You will see a Payment Strategy page with four boxes. Usually, the first box on the left is the most used in my opinion. Click all that apply—i.e. working, married, children, etc. Next it will ask you how soon or slow you would like to repay your loans. Keep in mind if you are on the PSLFP choice fast, look at the end date that it states 10 years or less. If the system guides you to an Income Contingent Plan, that means you have a FFEL loan and or Plus Loans that needs consolidating. If you choose nice and slow, you will be paying for 20 years to LIFE!. Note to everyone: If you work for a public sector and when you log in to see if you qualify for the public service loan forgiveness program but you may have FFEL or a Perkins loan, the system will tell you, you do not qualify. You do qualify, you have to consolidate those loans and convert them into Direct loans so they can be eligible for forgiveness.

If this has happened to you, call your lender and let them know that you are aware that you need to convert your non-direct loans so you can qualify for forgiveness. Do not consolidate by yourself if you are unsure.

Third, She needs to submit an Employment Verification Form to see if her place of employment is eligible for the public service loan forgiveness program.

Fourth, You may need to submit or resubmit an Income Driven Repayment Application to recalculate her income and select a plan that calculates 10% of your discretionary income. Ask the lender how much more accrual interests will be added to your principal if you apply for an Income Driven Repayment plan or switch plans and/or consolidate loans.

Example: Interests (I) = Principal(p) * Rate (r) * Time(t) .

Note: You will need to have your tax information ready to link to the IRS and Family Size.

 * If you work for the Government or a Nonprofit, the Standard Repayment plan is an option. However, make sure you look at the Revise Pay As You Earn and Pay As You Earn repayment options as it may be the best for you. To learn more, please refer to Item 3(a) on the Reference Page.

Any time you have a conflict with your lender, ask to speak with a supervisor. Write down the date, time and employee's ID number and keep a record in case you have to show proof for whatever reason. Be prepared to show documentation of your income such as paycheck stubs and your monthly obligations—or a financial disclosure form.

Chapter Four

The Cycle of Student Loan

Learning Activity

Goal of this lesson: To understand the cycle of your student loans so that you can determine where you are in the process.

Today's Tasks:

Review the Life Cycle of the Federal Student Loan Chart on the following page. Determine where you are and write down the details below. Be as descriptive as possible so you can refer to this information moving forward.

The Path of a Student Loan

When a student takes out a private loan, that is only the first step in a complicated process.

HOW IT WORKS

1 Students borrow money from the loan originators, mainly big banks and other institutions.

2 Banks bundle multiple loans and sell them to a depositor (in this case, National Collegiate Funding LLC).

3 The depositor in turn sells the loans to various trusts, like the National Collegiate Student Loan Trust.

4 The trusts employ a student loan servicer — in this case, American Education Services. Borrowers send their monthly payments to the servicer, which then sends money back to the trusts.

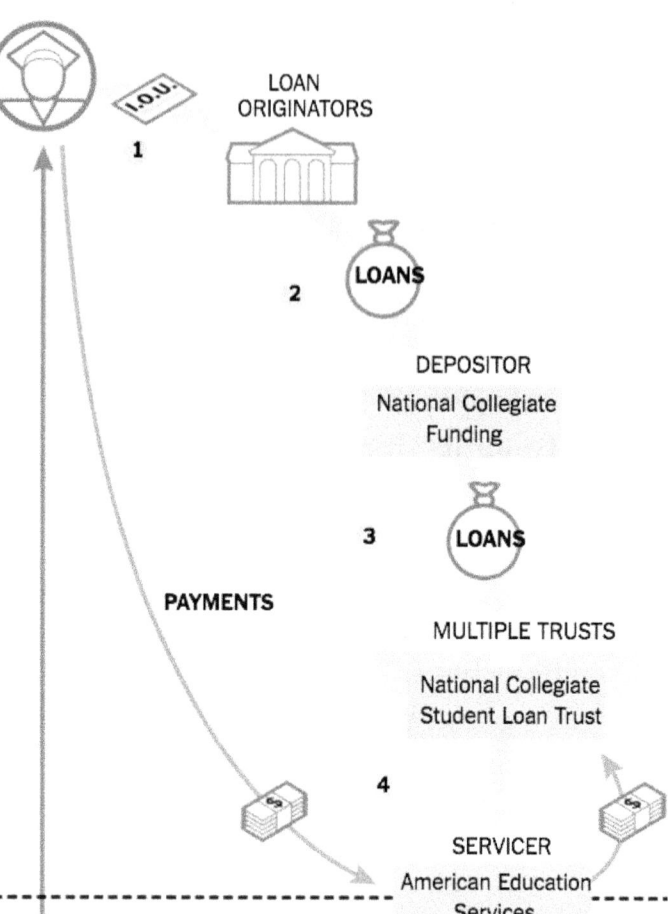

IF STUDENTS DEFAULT

5 American Education Services turns to U.S. Bank, based in Minneapolis, to collect on the debt.

6 U.S. Bank subcontracts the debt collection work to Transworld Systems, among other companies.

7 Transworld turns to its network of debt collection law firms, which may initiate lawsuits against

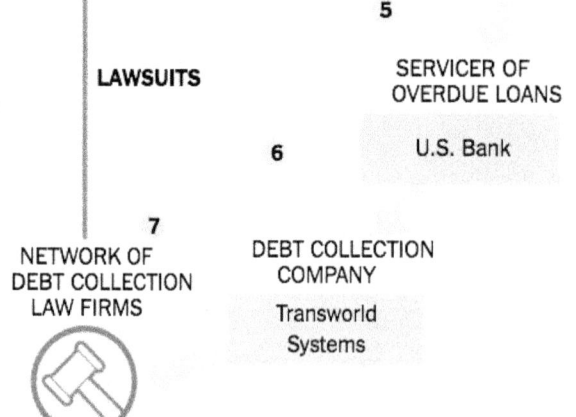

Write down where you are in the cycle:

_____

_____

_____

_____

_____

_____

_____

_____

_____

_____

_____

_____

_____

_____

_____

_____

_____

_____

_____

_____

_____

_____

_____

Chapter Five
Reflections

Learning Example

Reflections: Write down where you are using the chart below. (Example: I am in the process of repaying my loans with Navient. My interest rate is 4.6%. My monthly payment is $375.00.

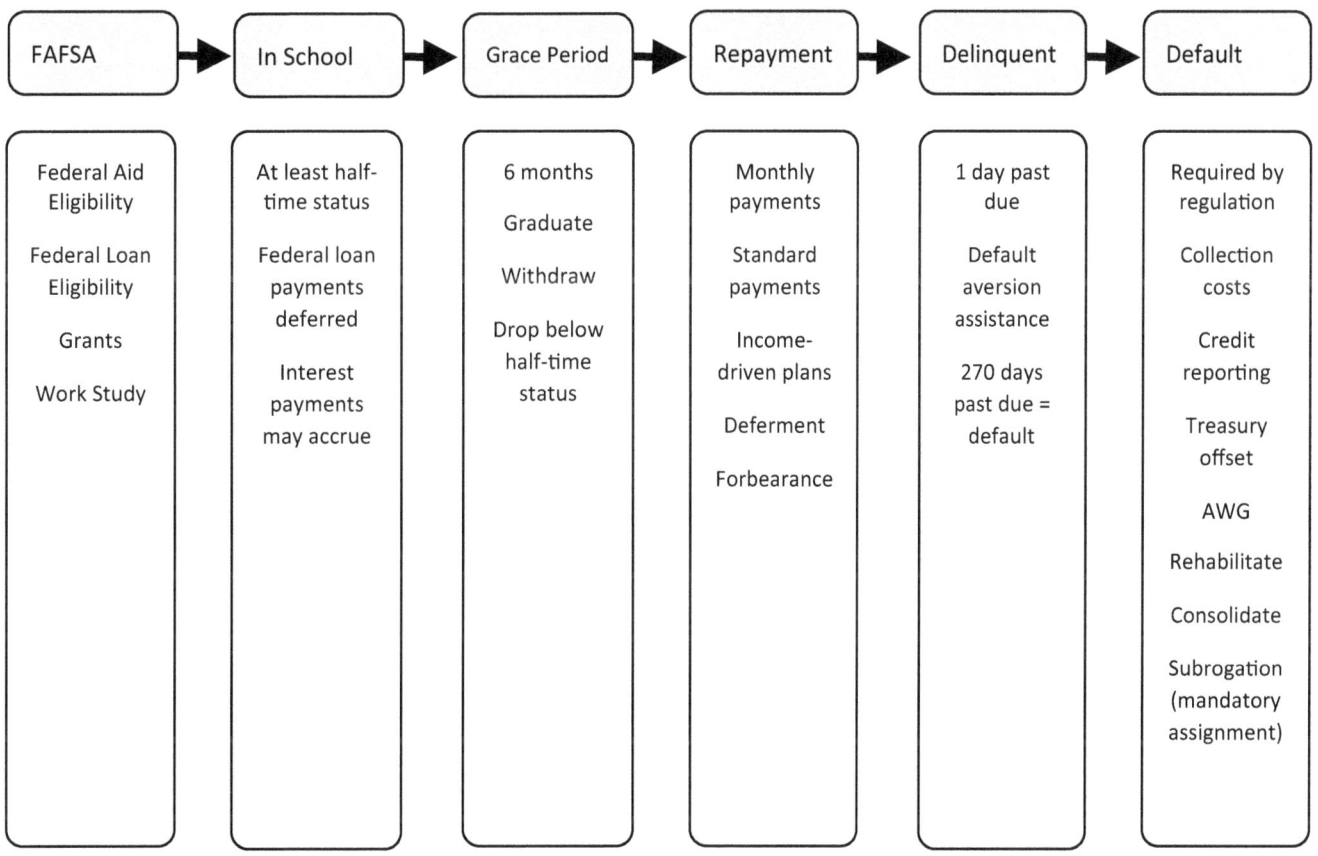

FAFSA →	In School →	Grace Period →	Repayment →	Delinquent →	Default
Federal Aid Eligibility Federal Loan Eligibility Grants Work Study	At least half-time status Federal loan payments deferred Interest payments may accrue	6 months Graduate Withdraw Drop below half-time status	Monthly payments Standard payments Income-driven plans Deferment Forbearance	1 day past due Default aversion assistance 270 days past due = default	Required by regulation Collection costs Credit reporting Treasury offset AWG Rehabilitate Consolidate Subrogation (mandatory assignment)

One day this cycle of student loan debt will be released.

Chapter Six

Your Student Loans

Learning Activity

Goal of this lesson: To understand the types of student loans that are listed on your NSLDS Worksheet.

Understanding the types of loans that you have is crucial in helping you to take steps to resolving your student loan debt. Without this knowledge your actions can make you ineligible for certain programs.

Your NSLDS contains all your loans, including grants and scholarships. It also indicates when your loans were disbursed, the amount that you were awarded and the current amount due with compounded interest.

Today's Tasks:

1. Review your NSLDS sheet and write down the type and number of loans that you have.

2. If you have several loans of the same type, just write it down once.

3. Next to each loan, write down how much you owe (see Lesson 3 of your course worksheet for the example).

4. Type of Loan, write the type of loans you have Direct, FEEL, Plus Loans, etc.

5. Loan amount, what is your balance?

6. The date your loans were disbursed .

7. Canceled amount if you have any.

8. Outstanding principal.

9. Outstanding interests.

Write below:

_____

_____

_____

_____

_____

_____

_____

_____

_____

_____

_____

_____

_____

_____

_____

_____

_____

I may owe this amount , however this debt will not control my life. I will put a plan in place to repay speedily. I AM FREE!

Loans

	Type of Loan	Loan Amount	Loan Date	Disbursed Amount	Canceled Amount	Outstanding Principal	Outstanding Interest
1	DIRECT STAFFORD UNSUBSIDIZED	$1,215	10/15/2013	$1,215	$0	$1,151	$49
2	DIRECT STAFFORD SUBSIDIZED	$2,785	10/15/2013	$2,785	$0	$2,595	$14
3	DIRECT STAFFORD UNSUBSIDIZED	$2,000	09/13/2012	$2,000	$0	$1,535	$82
4	DIRECT STAFFORD SUBSIDIZED	$5,500	09/13/2012	$5,500	$0	$5,104	$21
5	DIRECT STAFFORD UNSUBSIDIZED	$2,000	09/14/2011	$2,000	$0	$2,223	$192
6	DIRECT STAFFORD SUBSIDIZED	$5,500	09/14/2011	$5,500	$0	$5,018	$21
7	DIRECT STAFFORD UNSUBSIDIZED	$2,000	09/10/2010	$2,000	$0	$2,349	$203
8	DIRECT STAFFORD SUBSIDIZED	$4,500	09/10/2010	$4,500	$0	$4,123	$29
9	FFEL STAFFORD UNSUBSIDIZED	$4,712	08/31/2009	$4,712	$0	$5,052	$39
10	FFEL STAFFORD SUBSIDIZED	$788	08/31/2009	$788	$0	$0	$0
Total DIRECT STAFFORD UNSUBSIDIZED						$7,258	$526
Total DIRECT STAFFORD SUBSIDIZED						$16,840	$85
Total FFEL STAFFORD UNSUBSIDIZED						$5,052	$39
Total FFEL STAFFORD SUBSIDIZED						$0	$0
Total All Loans						$29,150	$650

As promised, we are going to begin taking steps toward getting certified for the Public Service Loan Forgiveness Program.

In this task, I want you to get a clear understanding of your student loans. Why? Having a deep understanding of where you stand and the type of student loans you have is necessary before pursuing the benefits of PSLF.

To get started, you will need your NSLDS Information sheet. Therefore, if you haven't already done so, download and print it so that you can complete this task.

Step 1. Create a FAFSA ID and Password through studentaid.gov

• The purpose of creating a FAFSA ID is so you can obtain student loan information.

• Creating the FAFSA ID and Password identifies you as the person eligible to receive

• Information through various financial aid programs. It serves as your legal signature.

Step 2. Log into the National Student Loans Data Systems via Studentaid.gov

- The National Student Loans Data Systems (NSLDS) is a tool that helps you keep track of how much aid you received.

- It also lists your loan status (paid or defaulted) and loan servicers.

- This information will help you determine which loans are eligible for forgiveness or other repayment programs.

Review the worksheet for the types of loans that you were awarded. Direct Loans are the loans that qualify for forgiveness. Having the right knowledge will help you communicate confidently with your financial aid representatives when managing your loans and applying for PSLF.

Please review Table 7 below from Studentaid.gov to help you understand the difference between Direct Subsidized and Direct Unsubsidized:

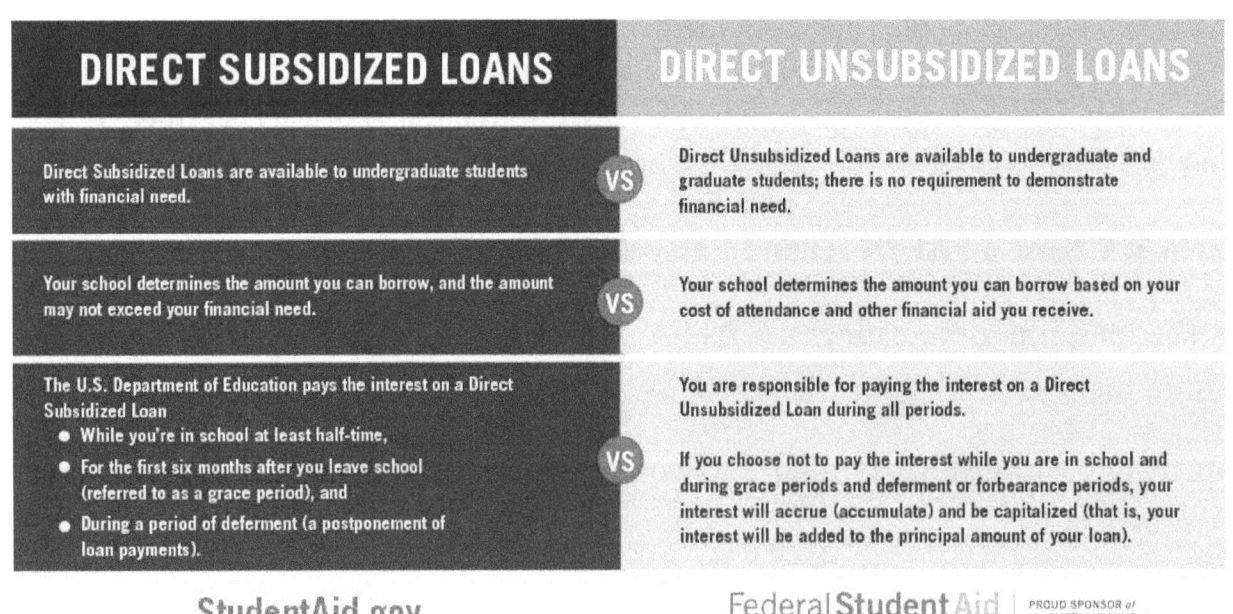

Chapter Seven
Next Module

Learning Activity: The Evolution of the PSLF Program

Goal of this Lesson: To determine which loans qualify for the PSLF Program

As you have seen on your NSLDS sheet, there are several types of loans. Some are eligible for the PSLF program while others are not. It is very important to understand which loans do and do not qualify so that you can take the necessary steps for certification. Always contact your lender when in doubt or need more clarity.

Today's Tasks:

1. Review the Loan Consolidation Sheet below.

2. Once you identify those loans that do not need to be consolidated, use a highlighter to identify those loans on the Sample NSLDS sheet.

3. Take the Quiz

Loan Consolidation Sheet 1

Consolidation Quiz 1:

	Type of Loan	Loan Amount	Loan Date	Disbursed Amount	Canceled Amount	Outstanding Principal	Outstanding Interest
1	DIRECT STAFFORD UNSUBSIDIZED	$1,215	10/15/2013	$1,215	$0	$1,151	$49
2	DIRECT STAFFORD SUBSIDIZED	$2,785	10/15/2013	$2,785	$0	$2,595	$14
3	DIRECT STAFFORD UNSUBSIDIZED	$2,000	09/13/2012	$2,000	$0	$1,535	$82
4	DIRECT STAFFORD SUBSIDIZED	$5,500	09/13/2012	$5,500	$0	$5,104	$21
5	DIRECT STAFFORD UNSUBSIDIZED	$2,000	09/14/2011	$2,000	$0	$2,223	$192
6	DIRECT STAFFORD SUBSIDIZED	$5,500	09/14/2011	$5,500	$0	$5,018	$21
7	DIRECT STAFFORD UNSUBSIDIZED	$2,000	09/10/2010	$2,000	$0	$2,349	$203
8	DIRECT STAFFORD SUBSIDIZED	$4,500	09/10/2010	$4,500	$0	$4,123	$29
9	FFEL STAFFORD UNSUBSIDIZED	$4,712	08/31/2009	$4,712	$0	$5,052	$39
10	FFEL STAFFORD SUBSIDIZED	$788	08/31/2009	$788	$0	$0	$0
Total DIRECT STAFFORD UNSUBSIDIZED						$7,258	$526
Total DIRECT STAFFORD SUBSIDIZED						$16,840	$85
Total FFEL STAFFORD UNSUBSIDIZED						$5,052	$39
Total FFEL STAFFORD SUBSIDIZED						$0	$0
Total All Loans						$29,150	$650

Table 5: Loans – NSLDS.gov

QUIZ 1: What Loans Do I Checkmark for Consolidation?

Knowing which loans to consolidate is crucial to navigating the consolidation process for the PSLF program. Test your knowledge before you start the process, and as a disclaimer, remember to call your lender when in doubt so you do not make a costly mistake.

Look at the chart and tell me which loan numbers should be checked for consolidation. Remember:

• The loans you checkmark are ones that you're telling StudentLoan.gov to consolidate.

• The loans you DO NOT checkmark are ones that you are not consolidating.

Choose an answer below:

1.   3,5,6

2.   1-8

3.   2,4,6,8

4.   9,10

Write your answers here for quiz #1: _____

Quiz 2: Consolidation

Loan ⌃	Current Balance ⌄	Interest R.
1-01 Stafford - Subsidized	$1,864.27	6.800%
1-02 Stafford - Unsubsidized	$3,965.14	6.800%
1-03 Stafford - Subsidized	$1,940.34	6.800%
1-04 Stafford - Unsubsidized	$4,050.14	6.800%
1-05 DL Consolidated - Subsidized	$8,388.24	6.300%
1-06 DL Consolidated - Unsubsidized	$9,364.72	6.300%
1-07 DL Consolidated - Unsubsidized	$2,989.46	6.250%
1-08 DL Consolidated - Subsidized	$2,792.83	6.250%
1-09 Direct Loan - Subsidized	$5,483.00	4.660%
1-10 Direct Loan - Unsubsidized	$7,915.32	4.660%
1-11 Direct Loan - Subsidized	$2,888.00	4.290%
1-12 Direct Loan - Unsubsidized	$10,376.89	4.290%
1-13 Direct Loan - Unsubsidized	$8,603.72	5.840%
1-14 Direct Loan - Unsubsidized	$21,392.58	5.310%

Choose an answer below:

1. Loans 1-4, and 9-14 should have a checkmark.

2. Only loans 1-4 should have a checkmark.

3. Only loans 9-10 should have a checkmark.

4. All of them should have a checkmark.

5. #9.

Write your answers here for quiz #2: _____

Did you get them both right? Remember to call your loan provider for assistance with consolidation. The answer for Quiz 1 is 2 and the answer for Quiz 2 is 4.

Disclaimer: Remember the choices you make are yours. In addition, call your loan provider if you do not understand how to proceed in loan consolidation and always make sure you have weighed your options before you consolidate your loans.

Ask the lender how much more accrual interests will be added to your principal if you apply for an Income Driven Repayment plan or switch plans and/or consolidate loans.

I am always available if you have questions, so feel free to email me at angela@finacialaidstartegist.com.

Loans

Please click on numbers in first column to see details including point of contact.

	Type of Loan	Loan Amount	Loan Date	Disbursed Amount	Canceled Amount	Outstanding Principal	Outstanding Interest
1	DIRECT STAFFORD UNSUBSIDIZED	$1,215	10/15/2013	$1,215	$0	$1,151	$49
2	DIRECT STAFFORD SUBSIDIZED	$2,785	10/15/2013	$2,785	$0	$2,595	$14
3	DIRECT STAFFORD UNSUBSIDIZED	$2,000	09/13/2012	$2,000	$0	$1,535	$82
4	DIRECT STAFFORD SUBSIDIZED	$5,500	09/13/2012	$5,500	$0	$5,104	$21
5	DIRECT STAFFORD UNSUBSIDIZED	$2,000	09/14/2011	$2,000	$0	$2,223	$192
6	DIRECT STAFFORD SUBSIDIZED	$5,500	09/14/2011	$5,500	$0	$5,018	$21
7	DIRECT STAFFORD UNSUBSIDIZED	$2,000	09/10/2010	$2,000	$0	$2,349	$203
8	DIRECT STAFFORD SUBSIDIZED	$4,500	09/10/2010	$4,500	$0	$4,123	$29
9	FFEL STAFFORD UNSUBSIDIZED	$4,712	08/31/2009	$4,712	$0	$5,052	$39
10	FFEL STAFFORD SUBSIDIZED	$788	08/31/2009	$788	$0	$0	$0
Total DIRECT STAFFORD UNSUBSIDIZED						$7,258	$526
Total DIRECT STAFFORD SUBSIDIZED						$16,840	$85
Total FFEL STAFFORD UNSUBSIDIZED						$5,052	$39
Total FFEL STAFFORD SUBSIDIZED						$0	$0
Total All Loans						$29,150	$650

1. 1-4

2. 1-8

3. 1-9

4. 9-10

The answer is 4.

If you have Parent Plus Loans or Graduate Loans, call your loan provider for consolidation assistance.

Chapter Eight

Qualifying for the PSLF Program

Learning Objective

Goal of this lesson: To understand the criteria for eligibility and steps to apply

Understanding how to navigate this program is crucial to getting your certification application approved. Making an error can result in potential ineligibility to the program. Please refer to Item 8(c) on the Reference Page to find an article from CNN in October of 2017 about a woman who thought her loans would be forgiven.

She is a teacher who spent 10 years making payments. Her $37,000 of student loan debt ballooned to over $70,000 with compounded interest, only to find out that she didn't have the right type of loans for PSLF and none of her payments counted.

Today's Tasks:

1. Find out what loans qualify for the Public Service Loan Forgiveness Program.

2. Learn the type of employment that will make you eligible for forgiveness.

3. Learn which server holds your loan while enrolled in the program.

**IF YOU ARE NOT INTERESTED IN APPLYING FOR THE PSLF PROGRAM, YOU DO NOT NEED TO COMPLETE THESE TASKS. THE

NEXT LESSON WILL TEACH YOU HOW TO USE THE REPAYMENT ESTIMATOR TO HELP REDUCE YOUR MONTHLY PAYMENT**

Qualifying Employment

What many people do not realize is that there is a wide variety of borrowers who qualify for PSLF beyond what Student Aid publishes on its website. On a very basic level, the people who can qualify are public service workers.

These are some of the job titles of people who work to serve the general public, listed on studentloans.gov:

• Teachers

• Doctors

• Government employees

• AmeriCorps and Peace Corps volunteers

• Employees of tax-exempt non-profits who offer the following services:

> • Emergency management

> • Military service

> • Public safety

> • Law enforcement

> • Public interest law services

> • Early childhood education

> • Public service for individuals with disabilities

- Public health

- Public education

- Public library services

- School library or other school-based service

- Liquor store

- Nonprofits

Check your local nonprofit agencies to see if they have openings if you are looking to become eligible to participate in the PSLFP.

Write down your local agencies here:

_____

_____

_____

_____

_____

_____

_____

_____

_____

_____

_____

_____

_____

Table 9: PSLF Employment Certification Form – StudentAid.gov/publicservice

PUBLIC SERVICE LOAN FORGIVENESS (PSLF): EMPLOYMENT CERTIFICATION FORM
William D. Ford Federal Direct Loan (Direct Loan) Program

PSLF ECF

OMB No. 1845-0110
Form Approved
Exp. Date 5/31/2020
PSECF - XBCR

WARNING: Any person who knowingly makes a false statement or misrepresentation on this form or on any accompanying document is subject to penalties that may include fines, imprisonment, or both, under the U.S. Criminal Code and 20 U.S.C. 1097.

ECTION 1: BORROWER INFORMATION

Please enter or correct the following information.
☐ **Check this box if any of your information has changed.**

SSN _____
Date of Birth _____
Name _____
Address _____
City _____ State _____ Zip Code _____
Telephone - Primary _____
Telephone - Alternate _____
Email (Optional) _____

ECTION 2: BORROWER AUTHORIZATIONS, UNDERSTANDINGS, AND CERTIFICATION

efore signing, carefully read the entire form. For more information on PSLF, visit **StudentAid.gov/publicservice**.

authorize:

1. My employer or other entity having records about the employment that is the basis of my request to make information from those records available to the U. S. Department of Education (the Department) or its agents or contractors.

2. The entity to which I submit this request and its agents to contact me regarding my request or my loans at any cellular telephone number that I provide now or in the future using automated telephone dialing equipment or artificial or prerecorded voice or text messages.

understand that:

1. To qualify for PSLF, I must make 120 qualifying payments on my Direct Loans while employed full-time by a qualifying

Employment That Does Not Qualify for PSLF:

People who **do not** qualify for PSLF include government contractors who work for profit and those who work for employers such as labor unions, partisan political organizations, for-profit organizations, and nonprofits that **are not tax exempt. Please pay special attention to tax-exempt status when working for nonprofits. The nonprofit MUST be tax exempt.**

You can learn more about qualifying job titles by referring to Item 8(b) on the Reference Page.

Don't work for a Nonprofit? Create Your Own.

Have you ever thought of becoming an Entrepreneur? Here is your chance! If you are interested in starting your own business, you can start a 501c3 and be eligible to qualify for loan forgiveness. I will provide you with more information on this later in the workbook.

Loans that Qualify for PSLF:

So, we have discussed the type of employment that qualifies. Let's focus on the loans that qualify. Direct loans are automatically eligible for PSLF. You <u>DO NOT</u> need to consolidate these loans for eligibility unless they are Direct Plus Loans, so they would need to be consolidated to be a part of the forgiveness process.

What to do with Non-Direct Loans

Non-Direct student loans can be consolidated into a Direct loan to make it eligible for the program.

FFEL Federal Family Education Loan, aka FFEL, are guaranteed-insured loans which include four components: Stafford Loans, Unsubsidized Stafford Loans, Federal PLUS loans and Federal Consolidation Loans. These loans are NOT qualifiable loans for the Public Service Loan Forgiveness Program which allows you to have your loans forgiven after 120 qualifying payments. A Perkins Loan can also cause you not to be eligible. You may want to pay this loan off or decide if you want to consolidate to make that loan a Direct Loan.

<u>Word of Knowledge:</u> Private Loans DO NOT AND WILL NOT EVER QUALIFY FOR PUBLIC SERVICE LOAN FORGIVENESS. Private loans are ones that you get from banks and other lenders.

> Now this is very, very important. There are many private financial institutions like banks and alternative lenders that will help you refinance federal student loans for a more affordable interest rate.
>
> The downside of refinancing your federal student loans with a private lender is that those loans are no longer eligible for PSLF and other government program benefits as with deferments or alternative plans.
>
> Be extremely careful to read the terms of all student loan solutions offered.

It is imperative that you know what you are doing ahead of making decisions. Before refinancing with a private lender, refer to Item 8(c) on the Reference Page.

If you have the following loan types below, check with your loan servicer to see if you need to convert them into Direct Loans:

These components below are listed on studentloans.gov. If you have any of the following federal student loans, check the date to see when you applied for them. You may need to consolidate them or turn them into Direct loans or inquire about their individual loan forgiveness before consolidation. If you have these loans check with your loan servicer before consolidation.

- Federal Family Education Loans (FFEL)

- Federal Perkins Loans

- Federal Supplemental Loans for Students (SLS)

- Parent Loans for Undergraduate Students (PLUS), if they are FFEL

- Auxiliary Loans to Assist Students (ALAS)

- Health Professions Student Loans (HPSL)

- Health Education Assistance Loans (HEAL)

• Nursing Student Loans (NSL)

• Loans for Disadvantaged Students (LDS)

If you got your loans *after* July 2014, you should already have Direct loans. Again, you DO NOT have to consolidate your Direct Loans unless they are Plus. When in doubt, call your provider and ask which loans qualify. Have them show you which ones can be consolidated and keep a record.

Loan Servicer That Qualifies for PSLF:

There is only one loan servicer that qualifies for the PSLF program. That servicer is **FedLoan Servicing PHEAA.org.** If you select a different service you are not in the PSLFP.

So, as I told you before, Direct Loans do not need to be consolidated unless they are Plus Loans. Check with your loan servicer. In addition, if your Direct Loan is with a servicer other than fedloanservicing.gov you need to enroll in an Income Driven Repayment (IDR) program, complete the Employment Verification form and transfer these loans to FedLoan Servicing.

Keep in mind that Direct Plus Loans must be on an Income Driven Plan to qualify for forgiveness. So if you have Direct Plus loans ask your lender to assist you with consolidating, Now the Direct Plus loans will be at 20% of your discretionary income, but if you choose Revise Pay as You Earn or Pay as You Earn, they will be calculated at 10% of your discretionary income. Discretionary income is the money that is left over after you have paid your monthly obligations. Look at these calculations:

1. **Calculate your daily interest rate (sometimes called interest rate factor).** Divide your annual student loan interest rate by the number of days in the year. 06/365 = 0.01643, or 0.016%

2. Calculate the amount of interest your loan accrues per day. Multiply your outstanding loan balance by your daily interest rate. $10,000 x 0.00016 = $32

3. Find your monthly interest payment. Multiply your daily interest amount by the number of days since your last payment. $32 x 30 = $9.60

Please do not *consolidate any* Direct loans that you already have, unless instructed by your loan servicer. A consolidation is when you take several debts and combine them into one new loan. Be aware, when you consolidate you will lose credit for the payments you have already made on those loans and you are starting over. Everyone's situation is different so contact your provider if you think you want to consolidate.

Consolidating, *instead of transferring,* your regular Direct loans to Fedloanservicing.org will erase the payments you have already made toward your 10-year PSLF commitment.

Again, this is incredibly important because I know someone who has experienced this firsthand. They consolidated Direct loans after having already made over 100 payments. The consolidation caused the payment history to be null and void. She had to start the payments all over again.

I know I said it already, but you only need to **transfer** your Direct loans to FedLoansServicing.org. Do not consolidate if you do not have Direct Plus loans. They can be tricky, so be sure you understand how to consolidate a Direct Plus Loan. If you have Direct Plus Loans, call your lender for help with consolidating, or I would be happy to assist you. I hope that this is very clear at this point.

Write Down Your Thoughts Here:

_____

_____

_____

_____

_____

_____

_____

_____

_____

_____

_____

_____

_____

_____

_____

_____

_____

_____

_____

_____

_____

I understand my options and if I have doubt I will call my loan servicer.

PAYMENT QUALIFICATIONS: 120 is the Magic Number

You need to make **120 qualifying payments** on eligible loans before you can obtain forgiveness. The 120 qualifying payments equal 10 years. Studentloans.ed.gov is the only entity that can approve your qualifying payments.

Qualifying payments happen when you work for an eligible employer for **30 hours a week**.

If you've worked for a qualifying employer and made payments on an eligible student loan since 2007, the loan payments you've made may qualify.

You read that right! You may find out that you are close to the 120 qualifying payments when you need to have your loans forgiven.

How amazing would that be?

DIRECT LOANS WITH ANOTHER SERVICER:

Direct Loans that are with other servicers need to be ***transferred*** to FedLoanServicings.org. This takes place during the Income driven process. During this process, you will also be prompted to ***consolidate*** your other federal loans (see qualifying loans earlier in this lesson). This is the correct time to consolidate your loans.

Other Federal Loans need to be consolidated to Direct Loans and then transferred to MyFedLoan.org in order to qualify for the PSLF program.

What Did You Learn?

In this lesson, you learned that there are 3 qualifying factors for the PSLF program. Let's review:

1. Work for a qualifying employer or start a 501c3 nonprofit.
2. Have existing or consolidated direct loans.
3. Requesting FedLoanPHEAA as your student loan servicer.

Write Your Notes Here:

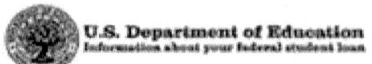

RESPONSE TO THE EMPLOYMENT CERTIFICATION FORM YOU SUBMITTED FOR THE PUBLIC SERVICE LOAN FORGIVENESS PROGRAM

Why We are Contacting You
We received the Public Service Loan Forgiveness (PSLF) Employment Certification Form you submitted and determined that the employers listed below are qualifying employers for the purpose of PSLF.

EMPLOYER NAME	BEGIN DATE CERTIFIED	END DATE CERTIFIED

Your employment qualifies you for participation in the PSLF Program for the certified employment time periods provided above. Note: If the dates of employment that you submitted on the form differ from those listed above, it may be due to overlapping employment periods, dates certified into the future, or periods of employment on or before October 1, 2007 (which do not qualify for PSLF).

What Happens Next
We will contact your current servicers to request a transfer of all of your U.S. Department of Education owned loans to us. This transfer will allow you to manage all of your loans in one location and closely track your progression toward PSLF. Please allow a few weeks for the entire transfer process to be completed.

Qualifying Payment Tracking for Public Service Loan Forgiveness
Once your servicer transfers your loans to us, we will calculate and provide you with notification of:

- The number of qualifying payments you have made during the qualifying employment period listed above,
- The total number of qualifying payments you have made during all periods of qualifying employment approved to date,
- The estimated number of payments that are still required, and
- The date you are expected to be eligible to apply for forgiveness.

After we receive your loans and calculate the number of qualifying payments you have made, keeping track of your progression toward PSLF is easy.

- Log in to Account Access at MyFedLoan.org
- Check your monthly bill
- Review the communication that we send you each time you submit a new ECF

Here is an approved Employment Certification Form for the Public Service Loan Forgiveness - Table 10

What's Next?

You will learn how to complete the PSLF Certification Process

Reflections:

_____

_____

_____

_____

_____

_____

_____

_____

_____

_____

_____

_____

_____

_____

_____

_____

_____

_____

_____

_____

_____

_____

Chapter Nine

Completing the PSLF Certification Process

Goal of this lesson: To take the steps necessary to successfully qualify for the PSLF program, the forgiveness will occur after 120 qualifying payments.

Remember, to be eligible to participate in PSLF, you must complete the employment certification form to see if your job is eligible, apply for IDR and make 120 payments.

If you have determined that you want to qualify for the PSLF program, you will need to complete the certification process, and I will provide you with the steps that you need to take.

**If you do not want to qualify for the PSLF program, I will provide you with steps to reduce your monthly payments.

Today's Tasks:

You will get the best results if you complete the tasks in order.

- Check to see if your employer qualifies for PSLF, or

- Take steps to create your own nonprofit if you are an entrepreneur or someone who doesn't work for a qualifying employer. Remember, only the U.S Department of Education can approve your nonprofit. Do not create a nonprofit for the sake of dealing with student loan debt. Create a nonprofit if you have a solution for solving problems and would like to share it with society. Having a nonprofit is like having a job. You must work 30 hours a week.

- View your loan type and see if you have DL, if not call your lender to help you consolidate the loans that do not apply for the PSLF. Be sure this is something you would like to do. Ask the lender how much more accrual interests will be added to your principal if you apply for an Income Driven Repayment plan or switch plans and / or consolidate loans.

Example: Interests (I) = Principal (p) * rate (r) * Time (t).

- Consolidate and transfer your debt to MyFedLoan.org

- Choose a repayment plan

- Fill out and submit your PSLF certification form

   o If you discover that you have already made 120 qualifying payments under an eligible employer (good for you!), submit the Employment Verification Form to confirm your eligibility, or

- Once you complete 10 years of service in the non-profit sector, you will need to take the final step to have your loans forgiven. Go studentaid.gov to submit the form.

A. How to Consolidate and Transfer Your Loans to MyFedLoan.org

A few reminders before you get started with this lesson:

- To protect your payment history, DO NOT CONSOLIDATE your Direct Loans

- All Direct Loans just need to be transferred, unless they are Plus or STAFFORD loans

- All PSLF loans are held with FedLoan Servicing PHEAA

- If your loans are currently being held by another servicer, you need to also transfer them to FedLoan Servicing PHEAA

Here are the steps you need to take to consolidate your loans or transfer them to MyFedLoan.org.

1. Pull out the NSLDS and your Course Worksheets so that you can follow your plan of action.

2. Go to StudentLoan.gov.

3. Input your FAFSA ID and password to log in.

4. Logging in will pull up all your information and student loans for consolidation.

5. Scroll to the bottom of the page and click on "Consolidate Your Loans". Check with your loan servicer if you are unsure on how to consolidate. If all your loans are Direct Loans, fill out the Income Driven Application and submit the Employment Verification Application. When you check the repayment tool estimator, look for Revise Pay as You Earn or Pay as You Earn. If you do not qualify for them, that means you have a loan that may need to be consolidated.

6. **UNCHECK** all the Direct loans on the list. The _checked loans_ are the ones that you'll be consolidating.

7. Follow the prompts and choose FedLoan Servicing as your new servicer (the unchecked Direct loans will transfer along with the loans that you consolidate).

8. Use the Your Income Tax tool information when asked. You can use the IRS tool to pull your tax forms electronically to make the process easier.

9. Put in your credit references.

10. Submit.

For help during this process

Call the Loan Consolidation Information Call Center and they can go over the steps with you.

** Be sure to make them aware that you _do not want_ to consolidate your existing Direct loans. I cannot express that enough.

- o I know I may sound like a broken record, but it's for a very good reason.

- o The key is understanding what you're doing BEFORE you call them so that they don't misguide you.

It's not uncommon for borrowers to call in and get misinformation. This is the very reason that Navient was recently sued. I am here to assist you and make sure this does not happen to you.

Understand that making errors here can potentially disqualify you for the program. My goal with this course is to empower you with information! When you call in, don't be afraid to explain what you need to happen and be firm, yet polite, in your requests.

What happens next?

- You'll get an email in 7 to 10 business days with a confirmation of receipt.

- It can take anywhere from 30 to 60 days for them to process the transfer.

B. Choose A Repayment Plan

When your transfer is complete, you'll be asked to select your preferred payment plan. If you are already in the plan of your choice, then just confirm your selection. Be sure to prepare yourself for this question by completing the Repayment Tool Estimator (see below).

What you need for this task:

- Your NSLDS worksheet

- Your FAFSA ID and password

- The Repayment Estimator Tool

- Your income tax return and link to IRS. If it will not link to the IRS. You will need to submit documents to your loan servicers. I.e paychecks stubs , W2's or Financial Disclosure form.

- Personal References

- Income base is 15% of your discretionary income

- Revise as You Earn and Pay as You Earn are 10% of your discretionary income

- ICR is 20% of your discretionary income
- Alternative repayment plan does not apply for forgiveness, but it is there for people who cannot afford their current loan payments. Ask your loan provider about this plan if your note is too high and you **do not** qualify for forgiveness and/or you are not interested in applying for forgiveness. You might find relief with the alternative repayment options.

This is important: Do Not Fall into This Trap:

Read the caption, loans cannot be forgiven instant enrollment. If you choose this plan have a strategy in place to pay your loans off. Start with the highest interests' rate and knock them off one at a time while paying this low monthly payment. Remember this plan is not a part of forgiveness. I would only use this plan to pay off debt. Not to stay in repayment for 25 years to life. The longer the debt, the more you back with interest. Remember to put extra funds in a savings account to pay taxes on the loans that may be forgiven in 25 to 30 years.

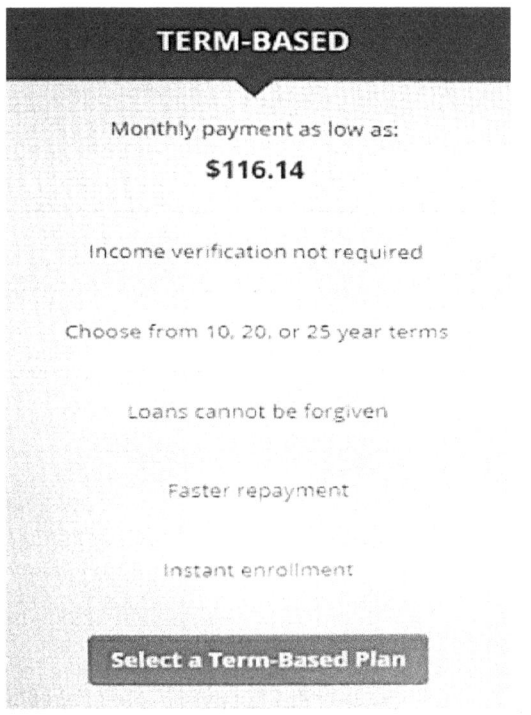

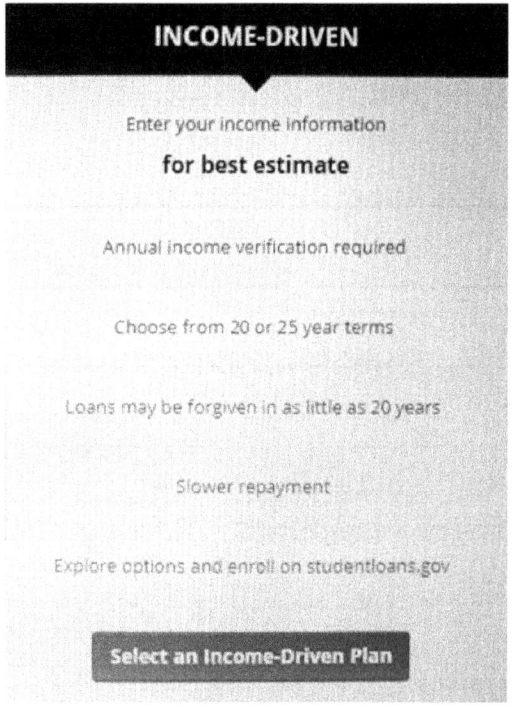

Remember when you log onto studentloans.gov or studentaid.gov Your loans may be higher until you fill out and or approved for an Income Driven Repayment plan. If you call your loan provider, they can assist you with an approximate payment amount. Choose wisely.

Remember, you can always upload your files by logging onto FedLoan Servicing:

- File Upload: - Sign in to MyFedLoan.org
- From the top right corner select "File Upload" –
- Select Income Driven Repayment –
- Upload this form and any additional documentation

Or use this mailing address:

U.S. Department of Education FedLoan Servicing

P.O. Box 69184

Harrisburg, PA 17106-9184

Sidebar: Always asks about Alternative Plans when you cannot afford to make monthly payments.

C. Getting Certified

Once your transfer is complete, you will need to complete the certification documents.

Employment certification looks like this and can be located online studentloans.gov:

PUBLIC SERVICE LOAN FORGIVENESS (PSLF): EMPLOYMENT CERTIFICATION FORM

William D. Ford Federal Direct Loan (Direct Loan) Program

OMB No. 1845-0110
Form Approved
Exp. Date 5/31/2020
PSECF - XBCR

PSLF ECF

WARNING: Any person who knowingly makes a false statement or misrepresentation on this form or on any accompanying document is subject to penalties that may include fines, imprisonment, or both, under the U.S. Criminal Code and 20 U.S.C. 1097.

SECTION 1: BORROWER INFORMATION

Please enter or correct the following information.

☐ Check this box if any of your information has changed.

SSN _____

Date of Birth _____

Name _____

Address _____

City _____ State _____ Zip Code _____

The purpose of the certification is to report the employers that you have worked for and the payments made towards PSLF. Always complete a renewal early to remain in compliance and so that you will not be charged with extra interests to your principal. Keep a lower payment by applying for an Income Driven Repayment Plan. Remember to keep your own copy as well. Here is a snippet of the Form:

Please do not confuse the Employment Certification Form with the Public Service Loan Forgiveness Form. They look similar:

Studentloans.gov will record information from your form and then update your qualifying payments each time. You will need to send an updated employment certification annually.

Remember, you must have a total of 120 payments to have loans forgiven. However, as long as you are submitting your yearly ECF you are placing your employer in the system to count your qualifying payments. And keep a copy of your records as well. Now remember to re-certify yearly, including your Income Driven Form if you need to and update on time to prevent any issues that may arise.

KEY: Always pay attention to the Form Approved Expiration Dates in the top right-hand corner. It will save you time, money and stress.

If you teach full time for five complete and consecutive academic years in a low-income elementary school, secondary school, or educational service agency, you may be eligible for forgiveness of up to $17,500 on your Direct Loan or FFEL Program loans. See StudentAid.gov for more information and a form you can fill out when you have completed your teaching service. Student Loans.gov.

If you owe more than 17,500, think about applying for the Public Service Loan Program instead. It may benefit you to have your loans forgiven as opposed to just having $5,000-$17,500 forgiven.

Common Reasons that Your Employment Certification Form Can Get Denied

Your goal is to be thorough with your approach in preparing for and applying for PSLF. This way you will decrease the chances of making a mistake that will cause your certification to get denied.

Mistakes that will impact your application include:

1. Not filling out the form completely and accurately.
2. Not having the proper employment.
3. Not starting the proper nonprofit with 501c3 or 501c4 tax exempt status.
4. Not recording the right dates or missing a date.
5. Incomplete applications.

My biggest piece of advice when completing this form is to look through every sentence and line of the form to make sure you've added the right information to your application.

Take your time!

This is What You Can Expect While You are in the PSLF Program.

Each year, you will receive a recertification reminder. You will need to complete this process to remain eligible for the program.

Once received, FedLoan Servicing will send you a statement of all the qualifying payments that you have made toward loan forgiveness while in the program. They will also advise you of the estimated date of forgiveness. Make sure you keep your own records; things have a way of not being there (wink, wink).

You can also review this information in your MyFedLoan.org account.

Be sure to keep a copy of ALL your paperwork, including your certifications and confirmations.

It's not unheard of for things to get lost in transition. You always need backup to prove your case if anything should happen.

What happens when you complete 120 payments?

Good question!

Remember, the certification for PSLF is not the application for actual forgiveness.

After making your 120 payments, you need to fill out *another* application to have your loans cleared. Download the PSLF Application for Forgiveness in the group files and save it for when you complete your payments.

The PSLF program went into effect in 2007 which means the first group of people who will be granted loan forgiveness will be getting it by the end of 2017.

The promise is that your student loans and interest compounding every day will be wiped clean.

You must still be working for an eligible employer when you turn in the final application. You will also need to complete Form 982 to possibly waive taxes on the amount of the loan that was forgiven. Otherwise, you will be responsible for paying the taxes if not approved by the IRS to have it waived. Note that President Trump has now waived this penalty. If you die or become totally disabled, you will not have to pay taxes on the debt.

Form **982** (Rev. March 2018) Department of the Treasury Internal Revenue Service	**Reduction of Tax Attributes Due to Discharge of Indebtedness (and Section 1082 Basis Adjustment)** ▶ Attach this form to your income tax return. ▶ Go to www.irs.gov/Form982 for instructions and the latest information.	OMB No. 1545-0046 Attachment Sequence No. **94**
Name shown on return		Identifying number

Part I   General Information (see instructions)

1	Amount excluded is due to (check applicable box(es)):	
a	Discharge of indebtedness in a title 11 case	☐
b	Discharge of indebtedness to the extent insolvent (not in a title 11 case)	☐
c	Discharge of qualified farm indebtedness	☐
d	Discharge of qualified real property business indebtedness	☐
e	Discharge of qualified principal residence indebtedness (**Caution:** See instructions before checking this box if debt was discharged after 2017.)	☐
2	Total amount of discharged indebtedness excluded from gross income	**2**
3	Do you elect to treat all real property described in section 1221(a)(1), relating to property held for sale to customers in the ordinary course of a trade or business, as if it were depreciable property?	☐ Yes ☐ No

Part II   Reduction of Tax Attributes. You must attach a description of any transactions resulting in the reduction in basis under section 1017. See Regulations section 1.1017-1 for basis reduction ordering rules, and, if applicable, required partnership consent statements. (For additional information, see the instructions for Part II.)

Enter amount excluded from gross income:

4	For a discharge of qualified real property business indebtedness applied to reduce the basis of depreciable real property	**4**
5	That you elect under section 108(b)(5) to apply first to reduce the basis (under section 1017) of depreciable property	**5**
6	Applied to reduce any net operating loss that occurred in the tax year of the discharge or carried over to the tax year of the discharge	**6**
7	Applied to reduce any general business credit carryover to or from the tax year of the discharge	**7**
8	Applied to reduce any minimum tax credit as of the beginning of the tax year immediately after the tax year of the discharge	**8**
9	Applied to reduce any net capital loss for the tax year of the discharge, including any capital loss carryovers to the tax year of the discharge	**9**
10a	Applied to reduce the basis of nondepreciable and depreciable property if not reduced on line 5. DO NOT use in the case of discharge of qualified farm indebtedness	**10a**
b	Applied to reduce the basis of your principal residence. Enter amount here ONLY if line 1e is	

Here is what $191,000 of Student Loan Debt Forgiveness Looks Like

Chapter Ten

If you do not wish to be a part of the Public Service Loan Forgiveness Program AND YOU JUST WOULD LIKE RELIEF

Step One:

Apply for an Income Driven Plan to lower your payments. If your payments are still too high, apply for this program. You may be eligible to pay $5.00 a month.

INCOME-DRIVEN REPAYMENT (IDR) PLAN REQUEST

OMB No. 1845-0102
Form Approved
Expiration Date:
8/31/2021

For the Revised Pay As You Earn (REPAYE), Pay As You Earn (PAYE), Income-Based Repayment (IBR), and Income-Contingent Repayment (ICR) plans under the William D. Ford Federal Direct Loan (Direct Loan) Program and Federal Family Education Loan (FFEL) Programs

IDR

WARNING: Any person who knowingly makes a false statement or misrepresentation on this form or on any accompanying document is subject to penalties that may include fines, imprisonment, or both, under the U.S. Criminal Code and 20 U.S.C. 1097.

SECTION 1: BORROWER INFORMATION

Please enter or correct the following information.

☐ Check this box if any of your information has changed.

SSN _____

Name _____

Address _____

City _____ State _____ Zip Code _____

Telephone - Primary _____

Telephone - Alternate _____

Email (Optional) _____

SECTION 2: REPAYMENT PLAN OR RECERTIFICATION REQUEST

It's faster and easier to complete this form online at StudentLoans.gov. You can learn more at StudentAid.gov/IDR and by reading Sections 9 and 10. It's simple to get repayment estimates at StudentAid.gov/repayment-estimator. If you need help with this form, contact your loan holder or servicer for free assistance. You can find out who your loan holder or servicer is at StudentAid.gov/login. You may have to pay income tax on any loan amount forgiven under an income-driven plan.

Step Two:

Find the repayment plan that gives you the best results for your income.

Examples:

IBR-15% of your discretionary income

Revised Pay as You Earn is 10% of your discretionary income

Pay as You Earn Is 10% of your discretionary income

Income contingent is 20% of your discretionary income (Plus Loans).

What is discretionary income and how is it used? Discretionary income is whatever is left after your taxes and mandatory household debt is deducted.

How are my loans calculated for my payments?

Step One:

Look up the Poverty Guidelines in your state using Item 10(a) on the Reference Page.

Step Two:

Multiply the Poverty guideline by your family size.

Step Three:

Use your previous year's tax return AGI (Adjusted Gross Income) and subtract the poverty guidelines for that year. This will give you the deduction calculations for discretionary income and give you the power to strategize a payment plan to fit your household needs.

Note: write down your calculation and a plan to reduce your loan amount. What type of financial savings will you implement to pay this debt off or keep up with your monthly payments on time?

Example: I will recertify on time yearly if I am in the PSLFP. I will make sure that my payments are set up on automatic withdrawal ensuring that I am making qualifying payments and saving 0.25% off the interest for using automatic systems, therefore lowering my monthly payments.

_____

_____

_____

_____

_____

_____

_____

_____

_____

_____

_____

_____

_____

_____

_____

_____

_____

_____

_____

_____

_____

_____

1. Calculate your daily interest rate (sometimes called interest rate factor).
Divide your annual student loan interest rate by the number of days in the year.
.06/365 = 0.01643, or 0.016%

2. Calculate the amount of interest your loan accrues per day.
Multiply your outstanding loan balance by your daily interest rate.
$10,000 x 0.00016 = $32

3. Find your monthly interest payment.
Multiply your daily interest amount by the number of days since your last payment.
$32 x 30 = $9.60

Calculate Your Daily Interest Below:

(2) your loans or income made you ineligible for the plan you selected.

Repayment Plan For Your Direct Consolidation Loan:To Be Determined

Other Repayment Plan Options
We want to make sure that you are aware of all of the available plans for your new Consolidation Loan. Review your options below to get an idea of the difference in payment amounts and total amount to be repaid for each of the plans.

Please keep in mind that we are **estimating** your payment amount and term for each of the plans, so the repayment details you receive may be different from the estimates in this letter. When your loan is disbursed, we will determine your repayment terms considering all of your account details at that time, and send you confirmation of your repayment plan details.

Good to Know: You can request to change your repayment plan at any time!

Repayment Plan	Number of Payments	Initial Payment	Maximum Payment	Total Interest to be Repaid	Total to be Repaid
Standard	360	$823.28	$823.28	$182,663.66	$296,374.20
Graduated	360	$709.76	$1,072.05	$182,861.42	$316,571.96
Extended Fixed	300	$882.05	$882.05	$130,899.31	$264,609.85
Extended Graduated	300	$709.77	$1,268.52	$151,986.43	$285,696.97
Income- Based Repayment*	To Be Determined	$348.73	To Be Determined	To Be Determined	To Be Determined
Income- Contingent Repayment*	To Be Determined	$667.47	To Be Determined	To Be Determined	To Be Determined
Revised Pay As You Earn*	To Be Determined	$232.48	To Be Determined	To Be Determined	To Be Determined

As part of an Income-Driven Repayment (IDR) plan, you are required to recertify annually. Since you will need to provide income and family size documentation each year, we are not able to provide you with all of the above details at this time.

Additional Repayment Plan Eligibility Information

You are not eligible for the plans listed below based on the loan or income requirements for that specific plan. For more information regarding the eligibility criteria for each of these plans, visit MyFedLoan.org/PaymentPlans.

• Pay As You Earn

_____

_____

_____

_____

_____

_____

_____

_____

_____

_____

_____

_____

_____

_____

_____

_____

_____

_____

_____

I have received my interest rates and I will make a plan to pay and save as much as possible.

Sign up to have your loans placed on an Income Driven Plan for lower monthly payments in most cases. Automation repayments will save you few coins on your monthly bill 0.25% off the interests' rate:

Apply for Income Driven Repayment to Lower Your Monthly Bill

Chapter Eleven

Tips

Defaulted Loans you can consolidate to come out of default and wage garnishments.

Disabled, you can have loans forgiven without tax applied after total disability discharge and you can be released from the debt and if you die, President Trump (2019) said you would not be responsible for taxes. "With the change in law to allow for disability discharge to be tax free, not only can disabled borrowers get student loan forgiveness, but they do not have to worry about negative impacts to their benefits as a result". For more information, please refer to Item 11(a) on the Reference Page.

If you cosign for someone's loans, you can have them to consolidate and you will be released from the debt. The borrower must be able to repay the loan without your help.

If your school closed while you were attending, or you had issues with your school catalog etc., call Borrowers of Defense in your state for assistance.

If you have private loans and you cannot afford to make the payments and your lender is not willing to assist you, contact Consumer Finance and they will assist you.

Military Service men and women, do not forget that your loans can be forgiven while you are protecting our country. Also, your rates are lower. Make sure you contact your lien holder more specific information regarding your personal account.

Closing

Many changes continue to evolve as it relates to student loan debt. My desire for you is that you do not stress over these loans and know that you can still purchase a home, car and have the American Dream once you understand your payment options and financial literacy. From this day forward read every line on any contract and ask about compounded interest. Know your credit score before applying for loans of any type. You have the power to break this cycle of Financial Aid Prison by learning and teaching the next generation about financial literacy, especially compounded interest. Do not forget to say your affirmations and review your NSLDS Sheet for clarity. Remember you are in control of your financial future. When in doubt call out for help by contacting your lien holder, logging onto studentaid.gov, click on estimate your payments and apply for Income Driven Plan. I am always available to assist you.

Connect with on Social Media Financial Strategist-Angela Howze or email me at angela@financialaidstrategist.com

Breakfree,
Angela Howze

No matter how big the door may be, I will
continue to share information to help you
break free of financial prison.

References

CHAPTER 1:

      Table 1: Student Preparation for Middle and High School

      https://ifap.ed.gov/dpcletters/attachments/20192020PellPaymentSchedule.pdf

      Table 2: Before College Checklist

      Chart 1. Studentaid.gov

CHAPTER 2:

      Item 2(a): www2.ed.gov/about/overview/fed/role.html

      Item 2(b): www.americaninno.com/boston/a-history-of-student-loan-debt

      Item 2(c): www.benefits.va.gov/gibill/history.asp

      Item 2(d): www.senate.gov/artandhistory/history/minute/Sputnik_Spurs_Passage

      Item 2(e): pellinstitute.org/downloads/trio clearinghouse

      Item 2(f): www.insidehighered.com/sites/default/server_files/media/

SLDT_ACT_2019

      Item 2(g): www.nasfaa.org

      Item 2(h): www.npr.org/sections/ed/2016/07/11/484364476

      Item 2(i): studentloans.gov/myDirectLoan/index.action

      Item 2(j): revealnews.org

      Item 2(k): www.forbes.com/sites/zackfriedman/2017/01/20/navient

CHAPTER 3:

      Item 3(a): Studentloans.gov/estimate

CHAPTER 4:

      Table 3: The Path of a Student Loan, New York Times, 2018

CHAPTER 5:

      Table 4: Life Cycle of a Federal Student Loan – Studentloans.gov – 2018

CPSIA information can be obtained
at www.ICGtesting.com
Printed in the USA
LVHW021936250821
696090LV00012B/959